My Gallipoli

Written by Ruth Starke

Illustrated by Robert Hannaford

For my father – R.S.

For Alison – R.H.

The characters portrayed in this book are both fictitious and real.
Where applicable, the Notes at the back of the book provide biographical details of those
who participated in the Gallipoli campaign and its aftermath.

With thanks to Bill Gammage, Adjunct Professor
at the Humanities Research Centre of the Australian National University.

This project has been assisted by the
South Australian Government through Arts SA.

**Government
of South Australia**

Arts SA

Working Title Press
An imprint of HarperCollins*Children'sBooks*, Australia

For Jos with love and thanks – J.

First published in Australia in 2015
by Publishing Design Studio Pty Ltd
This edition published in 2018
by HarperCollins*Publishers* Australia Pty Limited
ABN 36 009 913 517
harpercollins.com.au

HarperCollins*Publishers*
Level 13, 201 Elizabeth Street, Sydney NSW 2000, Australia
Unit D1, 63 Apollo Drive, Rosedale, Auckland 0632, New Zealand

A catalogue record for this book is available from the National Library of Australia

ISBN: 978 1 9215 0476 1

Designed and set in Cochin by Greg Holfeld, Panic Productions
Robert Hannaford used charcoal, watercolour and gouache for the illustrations in this book
Colour reproduction by Graphic Print Group, Adelaide
Printed and bound in China by RR Donnelley on 128gsm Matt Art

5 4 3 2 1 18 19 20 21

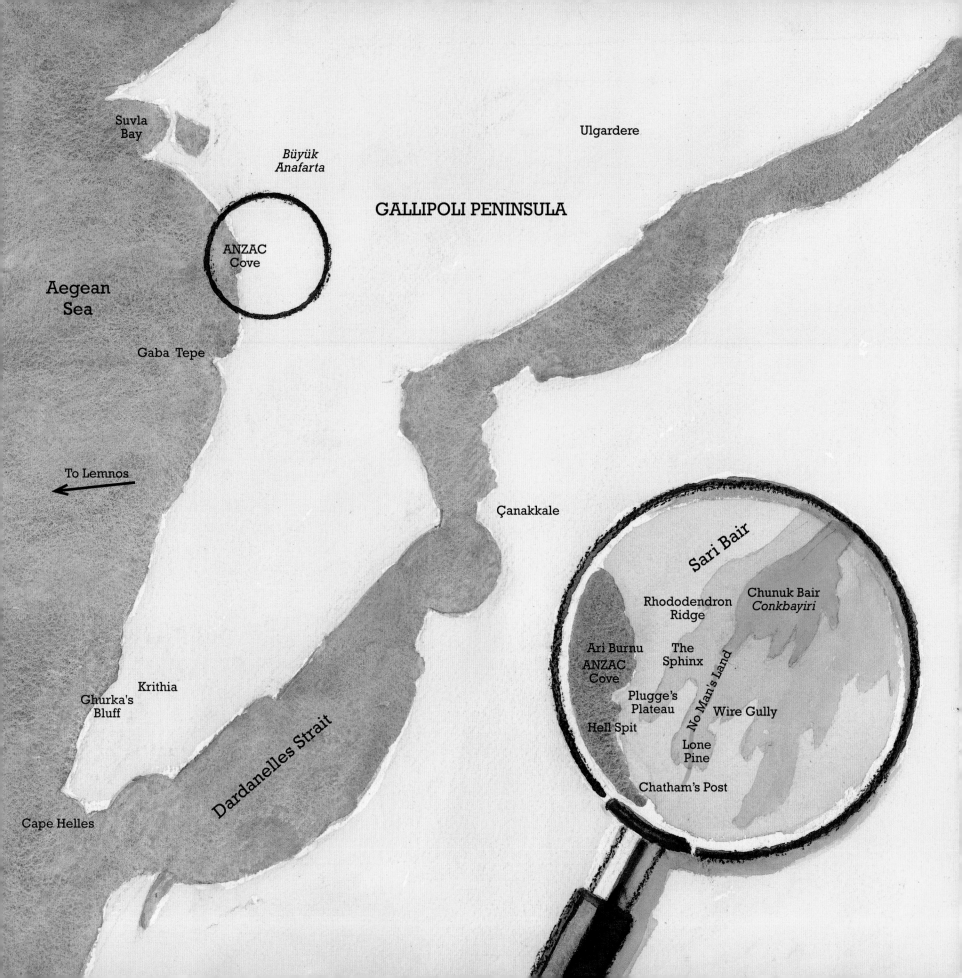

Suvla
Bay

Büyük
Anafarta

Ulgardere

GALLIPOLI PENINSULA

ANZAC
Cove

Aegean
Sea

Gaba Tepe

To Lemnos

Çanakkale

Krithia

Ghurka's
Bluff

Dardanelles Strait

Cape Helles

Sari Bair

Rhododendron
Ridge

Chunuk Bair
Conkbayiri

Ari Burnu
ANZAC
Cove

The
Sphinx

No Man's Land

Plugge's
Plateau

Wire Gully

Hell Spit

Lone
Pine

Chatham's Post

Hell Spit, Anzac Cove, November 1914

My name is Adil Sakin and my village, just north-east of here, is Büyük Anafarta. Like most of my friends, I'm a shepherd, but yesterday some army men came to the village and told us about the Great War and how we had to be soldiers. It sounds more exciting than looking after sheep, and of course I want to defend our village and my country. This land has belonged to us for hundreds of years and we will fight for it.

This Peninsula is my Gelibolu.

Anzac Cove, 25 April 1915

It's no easy thing to climb off a battleship in the dead of night and in full battle gear and get safely into a lifeboat. That's where I was, Midshipman Peter Burch RN, at 3 am on 25 April 1915, waiting in the number four tow to take the Australian troops in to shore. I was hoping the sea would be calm and the Turks asleep. Well, we got the calm water, but the Turks were wide awake.

When the keel grounded, men started jumping out, but many never reached shore. Shrapnel was raining down on us and I could see men all around me in the water, and I had two hit in my boat and no way of knowing whether they were dead or alive. On the beach it was all confusion, but my job was to row straight back to the *Prince of Wales* and pick up more troops. I did that all night until the sun was well up and you could see the bodies lying thick on the beach.

I never set foot on the Peninsula but this is my Gallipoli.

Anzac Cove, 25 April 1915

At the front you either survive or die. There is no escape. We are on high ground with a full view of the beach and the enemy is below us. Our heavy guns targeted their transport ships, and then we shelled their front line. We will stay here in our trench, with our rifles, and no one will leave his place until the enemy is driven back into the sea.

I am Private Jusef Demir of the 9th Division of the Turkish 5th Army, and this is my Gallipoli.

Anzac Cove, 25 April 1915

Nobody dreamed there would be so many casualties. We watched the dawn landing, and then they started coming aboard about 9 o'clock, on barges and boats, hundreds and hundreds of them, and all the time under enemy fire. The Turks even shot down stretcher-bearers. Their wounds are too awful to describe. I only wish my nursing skills were better; what I do seems so inadequate. By evening we had boarded 557 wounded and it was 2 am before I sat down to rest. The soldiers' poor, pale faces in the flickering ship's lights will haunt my dreams for years to come.

My name is Sister Ellen Walker and the hospital ship *Gascon* is my Gallipoli.

Cape Helles, 10–13 May 1915

My name is Rifleman Tul Bahadur Thapa and I am in the 6th Gurkha Rifles. Over 200,000 of us from Nepal joined the British Army when war was declared. Like all Gurkhas, I have been climbing mountains since I was a small boy, and I was very proud to be selected as one of the advance scouts to climb the bluff just west of Krithia, which the Turks commanded.

On 10 May, under cover of night, on our hands and knees we scaled the rocky cliff-face. As we neared the top the Turks started firing heavily at us and we had to retreat, but we did so with valuable reconnaissance information. In the early hours of 13 May a double company of the 6th Gurkha Rifles, under covering naval fire, captured the bluff. Our commander, Lieutenant-Colonel Bruce, ordered that in future it would be called Gurkha Bluff in honour of our victory.

This is my Gallipoli.

No Man's Land, 24 May 1915

My name is … well, it doesn't matter. The dead I buried today have no names either; the corpses were too far gone to recover identity discs. They'll be listed as missing, believed dead. We watched them for days, lying out there in the blazing sun, black and swollen and buzzing with green flies. The smell was terrible. An armistice was arranged, so both sides could bury their dead. We dug trenches and shovelled them in, twenty at a time: Aussies, Kiwis, Turks even … bodies that were too rotten to be moved across the line to the enemy's side. Harder to think of them as the enemy now. Reckon they're suffering just as much as we are, more perhaps. We traded cigarettes with them, and swapped biscuits for coins. Good fighters, the Turks. At 4.30 pm we'll put down our shovels and climb back into our trenches and the fighting will start all over again.

But for the thousands who lie under the earth of No Man's Land, this is their Gallipoli.

15

Too many bodies to give them proper burials. The trenches are full of the dead, huddled in heaps. The stench is awful. All we can do is drag the bodies into recesses and fill them in with earth. Three days and nights without rest and 647 men buried. So tired, and have consumed only three biscuits and six cups of tea in that time. When I do sleep I fear I will dream of dead men and burials.

My name is Chaplain Bill McKenzie and these graves are my Gallipoli.

My name is Private George Dawkins and I'm on stretcher duty. The graves are dug to take three bodies side by side. For the last trip we threw in the dirt to cover the two bodies, leaving one space vacant. While the chaplain was reading the service, I'm thinking: 'One click of a Turkish rifle and I could fill that third space'. And then I wondered whether their loved ones at home would ever hear how they were laid to rest here, on a Turkish hillside.

This will always be their Gallipoli.

What wretched cant it all is that they talk in the newspapers … I can't write about bayonet charges like some of the correspondents do … I can't write that it occurred if I know that it did not, even if by painting it that way I can rouse the blood and make the pulse beat faster …

But war correspondents have so habitually exaggerated the heroism of battles that people don't realise that the real actions are heroic … There is horror and beastliness and cowardice and treachery, over all of which the writer, anxious to please the public, has to throw his cloak – but the man who does his job is a hero. And the actual truth is … that there is a bigger proportion of men in the Australian Army that try to do it cheerfully and without the least show of fear than in any force or army that I have seen in Gallipoli. The man who knows war knows that this is magnificent praise. The public can never know it.

This is my Gallipoli.
C.E.W. Bean, Official War Correspondent

THE DARDANELLES

LANDING OF THE AUSTRALIANS

HOW IT WAS EFFECTED

"NOTHING STOPPED US"

Reuter's correspondent at Cairo has telegraphed the first report of the actual fighting during the landing of the Australasian troops at Gaba Tepe, on the western shore of the Gallipoli Peninsula last week. It reveals many stories of dash and courage.

When approaching the shore the Australians and the New Zealanders jumped from the boats into water that was often neck deep, and waded to land. They found the Turks occupying the ridges, and took three of these in succession in a running fight, extending over a length of three miles.

One Australian said afterwards:— "Nothing stopped us. Our big lads lifted some of the Turks on the end of their bayonets, and the other Turks ran screaming and howling in fear. After the first rush others of our men came up, and helped to storm the ridges and to consolidate new positions.

"The enemy's fire from shrapnel, machine guns, and rifles was terrific throughout; but our men never wavered.

"Our casualties were heavy, but very many of the wounds are slight, and the men will reappear in the fighting line in a few weeks."

The wounded state that the Red Cross worked magnificently. The ambulance men were under fire, the Turks making a dead set against them, and shooting them down mercilessly.

The Turks' losses were enormous, the bayonet rushes of the Australians and New Zealanders causing great slaughter.

It has been established that the Turks used dum-dum bullets.

sisted by a thick mist and a rainstorm, intending to make it impossible for the British transports to land supplies under cover of night.

The French, on Wednesday (April 28) landed at Morto Bay, on the European shore at the entrance to the Straits, astride of the roads leading to Krithia, three miles inland. The Turkish guns replied from a position one mile behind Krithia, which the naval guns set on fire.

Fight for Achi Baba.

A height named Achi [Baba], one mile and a half to [...] dominates the region [...] obstacle to the Allies [...]

By 1 o'clock on [...] were across a penin[...] Krithia, and shrapnel [...] Baba, which the [...] on the European [...] Erekeui Bay, on the [...] shelling.

Krithia was prac[...] fall, and the Tur[...] reply, except wh[...] in shore. The [...] the Turks in a fe[...]

During Wedn[...] the northern [...] view to the [...] su[...] sh[...] ke[...] fr[...]

AUSTRALASIANS

GLORIOUS ENTRY INTO WAR.

HISTORIC CHARGE.

BRILLIANT FEAT AT GABA TEPE.

The story of how the Australasian troops landed at Gaba Tepe, and made good their footing, in the face of the Turkish fire and subsequent counter-attacks, is vividly told by Mr. Ashmead Bartlett.

The work of the covering force was splendidly carried out, and Mr. Bartlett says there has been no finer feat of arms in this war than that of the Colonial troops.

Operations, according to an official statement, are now being pressed on under highly satisfactory conditions, though the enemy is offering stubborn resistance.

The eighth casualty list issued by the Defence Department [...]tained the name of one additional [...]ied from wounds.

A GREAT BATTLE

A GENERAL ADVANCE MADE.

DESPERATE FIGHTING FOR TRENCHES.

REPORT FROM GENERAL HAMILTON.

MELBOURNE, June 6.

The following cable message was received to-day by the Minister of Defence (Senator Pearce) from Sir Ian Hamilton:

"The Turks having heavily bombarded a small fort that the French had captured in front of their extreme right and breached it in the north-east angle, launched an infantry attack against it, which was repulsed. About the same time they set fire to scrub in front of the left centre of the 29th Division, and attacked, but without success.

"On the morning of the 4th inst. I made a general attack on the Turkish trenches in the southern area of the peninsula, commencing with a heavy bombardment by all guns, including two battleships, two cruisers, and several destroyers, with four inch [...]

STORY OF THE LANDING

AUSTRALIANS FACE DEATH

"THEY ROSE TO THE OCCASION"

Mr. Ellis Ashmead-Bartlett, the war correspondent who was chosen to represent the British press at the Dardanelles, has telegraphed his first story of the operations, especially with the landing of the Australian and New Zealand troops at Gaba Tepe, on the western shore of the Gallipoli Peninsula, having had the advantage of witnessing it. Mr. Ashmead-Bartlett represented the London "Daily Telegraph" during the Balkan wars, when his stirring and reliable messages brought him to the very forefront of war correspondents.

Wire Gully, 8 June 1915

The trick is not to be seen against the horizon. You can crawl out of any trench or hole provided the back parapet is high enough not to silhouette you. Then you go flat like a snake on the inside of your knees, inside of knuckle of big toes and inside of elbows, and not on your kneepads and palms. When you come to a rise, again, don't get up but go over it like a snake, bending your body over the top of the bank, your chest almost scrubbing it all the way. No rifle. Your job is to see, not to shoot, unless you're at close quarters and then a revolver's the weapon for that. A rifle, especially with a bayonet fixed, simply shows you up.

My name is Lance Corporal Harry Freame and I'm a scout in the 1st Battalion, NSW.
This is my Gallipoli.

Chatham's Post, June–September 1915

Every time I feel sorry for the Turks I remember how their snipers picked off our officers during the early days of the landing, and I harden my heart. With my spotter, I take up my possie early while it's still dark, and I don't move until after dusk. I use a Lee Enfield .303 rifle, but I never fire at stretcher-bearers or Turks trying to rescue wounded comrades. On the other hand, if I spot an injured Turk, I'll shoot and put the poor cuss out of his agony. The boys call me the Murderer, but you have to be tough to be a sniper, and I don't lose any sleep over what I do. The regimental records credit me with 150 confirmed kills, but I'd say the true tally is twice that number. The Turks sent their champ, Abdul the Terrible, to hunt me down but I fired first and got him.

My name is Trooper Billy Sing of the 5th Light Horse, and this is my Gallipoli.

Chunuk Bair, 6–8 August 1915

To the Australian and New Zealand Army Corps my name is Private Andrew McBain, No. 3455, Auckland Mounted Rifles, but to my mates I'm just Andy. There aren't many of them left. Mates, that is.

On 6 August we were ordered to capture Turkish positions on Chunuk Bair, one of the peaks above Anzac Cove. Just getting to the foothills took all night, and scrambling through gullies and up scrubby slopes in the pitch black was no picnic, not to mention clearing the Turks out of the trenches with our bayonets.

By dawn of 7 August we were on Rhododendron Ridge. Chunuk Bair was only about 500 metres away and seemed undefended. Why didn't we keep going and take it? Someone said we were waiting for more men. Anyway, by the time the order to advance was finally given the Turks had dug in with machine guns, and were ready to defend the summit.

And they did. Well, it was broad daylight. They could see us coming. Two hundred of us Aucklanders killed in twenty minutes, most of the rest of the battalion wounded. The bullets flew past so close I could feel the air move; zip, zip, zip in my ears like a whisper. We tried to take cover in a shallow trench and the Turks shot at us from above all day long while we waited for reinforcements that never came. My best mate Frankie was hit during the advance, and with dozens of others lay out in the blazing sun all day, with little food and water and no way to bring them in until dark. I could hear him reciting The Lord's Prayer.

Just before dawn the next morning we saw the Wellington Battalion take the peak, but this is my Gallipoli.

Chunuk Bair (Conkbayiri), 4.30 am, 10 August 1915

I warned that the steep slopes and valleys below Conkbayiri would not stop an Allied advance. I was not believed and our defences were not strengthened. But even I did not guess that the attack would come at night … The battle raged for two days and the enemy has taken the peak. The dead lie everywhere. My officers are tired and want to sleep, but there must be no rest. To wait is to give the advantage to the enemy. If we attack at dawn, before their warships and machine guns can open up, we have a chance of retaking Conkbayiri.

The blanket of night has lifted. Now is the hour for the attack. My exhausted troops are assembled below the peak. I go forward and address them: 'Soldiers! There is no doubt we will defeat the enemy. But do not rush into battle. Let me take the lead. When you see me wave my whip, all advance together!'

I take up my position at the front of the assault line and raise my whip.

I am Lieutenant-Colonel Mustafa Kemal and this is my Gallipoli.

Chunuk Bair, 10 August 1915

On 9 August, those of us Aucklanders who were left – about a hundred, I reckon – were sent to reinforce the Wellington Battalion who were fighting off a Turkish attack on Chunuk Bair and had been mostly slaughtered in the process. The earth was red with blood, but together with British reinforcements we held the peak for another twenty-four hours before a fresh wave of Turks on 10 August swept us off the summit.

They reckon about 2,000 Allied casualties all up; my mate Frankie was one of them.

Chunuk Bair will always be his Gallipoli.

Lemnos, 4 September 1915

Dear Mum and Dad,

You can stop worrying about me now as I'm out of the fighting and in hospital on the island of Lemnos, being looked after by bonzer Aussie nurses. When supplies ran out they tore up their own clothes for bandages. Just like in the trenches, water is in short supply so I am growing quite a beard. I am not feeling too well at present but my injuries are not half as bad as those of some of the brave lads here. We can hear the guns from the Peninsula, but for now this is my Gallipoli.

Your loving son,
Jack

31

Suvla Bay, November 1915

Never been so hungry and cold in my life. Last night there was a blizzard, something we don't get in Queensland. When war was declared, me and my mate Walt enlisted right away. We were both crack riders on Coorabulka cattle station, and I reckon that's why they took us for the 5th Light Horse Regiment, even though we're Aborigines. But horses are no use here, and we had to leave them in Egypt. People back home said, 'Why'd you enlist to fight a white man's war, Jimmy?' I said, 'It's my country too'. The men in my mob have always been warriors. And on the battlefield everyone's equal, white and black, we fight side by side. Equal pay, too, six shillings a day! We don't get that in Queensland neither!

My name is Trooper James Lang, and this is my Gallipoli.

Anzac Cove, 16–17 December 1915

December 16: Anzac looks extraordinarily empty – the beach quite deserted. We have burnt our papers, and there will be very little left to the Turks to interest them … The men aren't sorry to leave – not most of them. They regret leaving their comrades buried here, and the number of demands for timber for graves has been enormous. I see solid-looking crosses going up everywhere over the old biscuit box ones.

December 17: I smashed my home-made furniture myself and put a knife through the waterproof sheets when I left my dugout. Somehow I don't like to think of that furniture as a curiosity in some Turkish Officer's home.

My name is Charles Edwin Woodrow Bean, and for eight months this has been my Gallipoli.

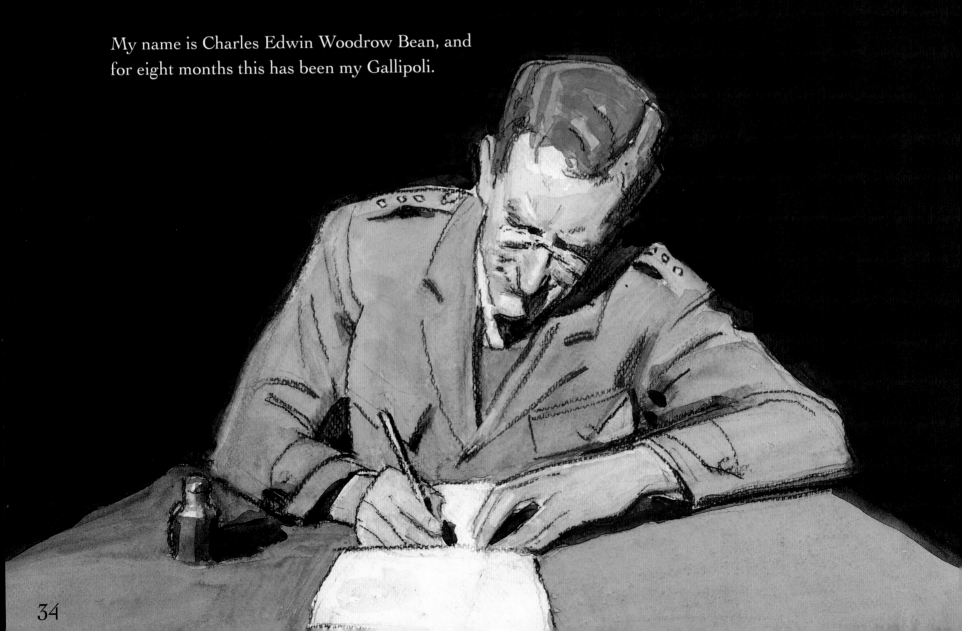

Suvla Bay, 17 December 1915

Please do not think that service in the Mule Corps is not a soldierly activity. We and our animals share in the hardships and dangers, delivering ammunition and supplies to the trenches, or carrying guns to and from different positions. Now, after eight months, all that has stopped. We are evacuating the Peninsula. We have selected fifty of our noisiest squeaking carts for the last convoy, so the Turks will think everything is as normal. But when dawn breaks tomorrow, Anzac will be deserted.

My name is Badhur Singh. I am a driver with the Indian Mule Cart Corps, headquartered at Suvla Bay. This is my Gallipoli.

Melbourne, November 1915

Dad cried when he first saw our Jack. 'How's he going to work now?' he wanted to know. I worried more about what lass would want to marry him, though I never said a word to Jack, of course. He's a changed man from the strapping young lad who marched off to fight for the Empire. His letters home were always so cheerful, never a word about how bad his injuries were, and the telegram told us nothing.

He doesn't talk much about what it was like over there, but for now and for the rest of my life, this is my Gallipoli.

Lone Pine, Gallipoli, December 1918

At first I thought the land was covered with a light layer of melting snow. And then we approached and saw that over the former trenches lay the bare white bones of those who had fought and fallen here over three years ago. In places the bones were so thickly clustered we had to tread upon them as we passed.

My job with the Graves Registration Unit is to help identify and rebury the remains of Allied soldiers, and chart the graves and cemeteries. Sometimes individual identification is impossible here, and then the trenches and tunnels, and the bones they contain, are filled in as a mass grave.

My name is Lieutenant Cyril Hughes and this is my Gallipoli.

Anzac Cove, Gallipoli, 1919

I did the first sketches today, looking up at the cliffs above Anzac Cove. It is a disturbing and melancholy landscape, and I am much affected by the constant unearthing of bones and bodies that is going on around me.

My name is George Lambert, I am an official Australian war artist, and this is my Gallipoli.

Ari Burnu, Gallipoli, 1988

My brother, Adil Sakin, fought and died here in May 1915. He was not yet eighteen, my father's eldest son. I was too young to fight, but after the war I helped build these cemeteries. There were many of us – Greeks and Russians as well as Turks – led by an Australian, Lieutenant Hughes. The stone came from a quarry at Ulgardere, the same stone that built the walls of Troy.

This is a place for heroes. This is my Gallipoli.

Lone Pine Cemetery, 1990

My name is Kelly Gillison and this is where my great-grandfather is buried. Well, 'believed to be buried', like the stone says. So many names. All of them so young. The world seems at peace here. It's hard to imagine what it must have been like for them back then. I'm filled with sadness, but I'm glad I came. I've walked across the same earth that my ancestor fought on.

This is my Gallipoli now, and I will never forget.

43

We will remember them.

Pages 4–5

Gelibolu, also known as Gallipoli, is the name of a town and a district in Çanakkale Province. In 1914, Turkey's army was shattered and the country was effectively broke. Its leader, Enver Pasha, saw the war in Europe as an opportunity for Turkey to regain lands that had been lost to Russia and decided to take Turkey into the war on the side of Germany. Most new army recruits came from rural peasant backgrounds and had little or no formal education and little knowledge of the world.

Pages 6–7

At dawn on 25 April 1915, the Gallipoli campaign began. The first wave of 1500 men disembarked from three British battleships, the *Prince of Wales*, the *Queen*, and the *London*, into twelve tows, each comprising a steamboat, a cutter (30 men), a lifeboat (28 men), and either a launch (98 men) or a pinnace (60 men).

Pages 8–9

The invading Anzacs were confined to the beach of Anzac Cove and a small area of the cliffs. Crucially, they did not hold the high ground, and even though the Turks were outnumbered, their response was swift, effective and deadly. During the eight months of conflict, the Anzacs' position on the Peninsula did not substantially change.

Pages 10–11

By the end of 1914 around 300 nurses from the Australian Army Nursing Service had left Australia for Egypt, but serving on a hospital ship was the closest any of them came to the fighting during the Gallipoli campaign. Over the nine months following the 25 April landing, the *Gascon* would transport over 8,000 wounded and sick soldiers between the Peninsula and the various field hospitals.

Pages 12–13

The capture of the bluff in May 1915 was the first major operation of the 6th Gurkha Rifles since landing at Cape Helles in April. In August 1915, at Sari Bair, the 6th Gurkhas were the only troops in the whole campaign to reach and hold the crest line and look down on the Dardanelles Strait, which was the ultimate objective. They held the position for three nights and two and a half days.

Pages 14–15

On 24 May 1915, a nine-hour armistice, or ceasefire, was declared so Anzacs and Turks could bury their dead and thus remove the nauseating stench that made life in the trenches almost unbearable. Identification of bodies was often impossible because the fibre identification discs issued to British and Allied forces during WW1 disintegrated over time.

Page 16

Chaplain Major William McKenzie (1869–1947) of the Salvation Army was chaplain to the 1st Infantry Brigade, AIF, and went ashore with the troops at Anzac Cove. Known as 'Fighting Mac', he was awarded the Military Cross, a rare honour for a military chaplain.

Page 17

Officially, the whole Gallipoli operation resulted in 26,111 Australian casualties, including 8,141 deaths. The true figure can never be calculated because of the conditions under which the campaign was fought. Turkish casualties were about 218,000, including 66,000 deaths.

Page 18

Charles Edwin Woodrow Bean (1879–1968), usually identified as C.E.W. Bean, was the official war correspondent with the AIF. He landed at Anzac Cove on 25 April and remained on the Peninsula for most of the campaign. He returned to Gallipoli with the Historical Mission in 1919. The words here are taken from his diary entry of 26 September 1915, at Anzac Cove.

Page 19

The first news of the landing on 25 April was published on 29 April in daily newspapers around Australia. The tone was overwhelmingly victorious, and the heroic qualities of the Anzacs were praised. Operational details were brief and the casualties were not specified.

Pages 20–21

Henry 'Harry' Freame (1880–1941) was born in Osaka, Japan, to a Japanese mother and Anglo-Australian father. Freame landed at Anzac Cove on 25 April with D Company, 1st Battalion, and was later awarded the Distinguished Conduct Medal (DCM) for his bravery during those first confusing days. Freame's job was to go ahead of the main force to collect information about the Turkish positions: Charles Bean called him 'probably the most trusted scout on Anzac'. This portrait is based on a photograph Bean took of Freame at Wire Gully, 8 June 1915. (Australian War Memorial Neg. No. G01030A.)

Pages 22–23

The son of a Chinese father and English mother, William Edward Sing (1886–1943) was a kangaroo shooter from Queensland who regularly won prizes for his shooting. He enlisted as a Trooper with the 5th Light Horse Regiment shortly after the outbreak of war, when a recruitment officer chose to overlook his Chinese ancestry. He became the crack shot of the Anzacs, and in March 1916 he was awarded the DCM.

Pages 24–25

The battle of Chunuk Bair was literally the high point of the New Zealand effort at Gallipoli, but Auckland Mounted Rifles' casualties were so high that the unit almost ceased to exist. The Wellington Battalion reached the summit before dawn on 8 August.

Pages 26–27

Mustafa Kemal (1881–1938) commanded the 19th Division of the Turkish 5th Army during the Gallipoli campaign. At Chunuk Bair he led his troops to win the most decisive battle of the Gallipoli campaign. After the war Kemal became the first President of Turkey and was given the surname 'Ataturk', which means 'Father of the Turks'. His words to his troops before the battle of Chunuk Bair are recorded in the memoirs of many of his associates.

Pages 28–29

The Wellington Battalion, reinforced by what was left of the Auckland Mounted Rifles and two British battalions, held the summit of Chunuk Bair for 24 hours against repeated attacks. The casualties were appalling. Today a New Zealand memorial stands on the summit. It has a narrow slit through which the rising sun shines on 8 August.

Pages 30–31

Lemnos, called Limnos today, is a small island (477 square miles or 123,500 hectares) in the North Aegean Sea, about 80 kilometres from the Dardanelles. Ships for transport and supply were able to anchor at the large harbour at Mudros. There were no suitable buildings, so tents were used as hospitals, and when beds ran out men had to lie on the ground. Sanitary arrangements were primitive and water – condensed seawater – was only available by the bucket and rationed.

Pages 32–33

It is estimated that at least 400, and possibly as many as 800, Indigenous Australians fought in WWI. Accurate numbers are difficult to establish as the Army did not record the ethnic origins of those enlisting. By law, Aborigines were prevented from enlisting unless they were substantially of European background, but nonetheless many were accepted.

From mid-November onwards the weather on the Peninsula began to deteriorate, culminating in a blizzard on the night of 26 November. It was the coldest winter for decades, and one for which the authorities had not prepared. At Suvla more than 200 British troops died of exposure, and over 3,000 Anzacs were evacuated with frostbite or trench foot.

Page 34

By 20 December the evacuation of Anzac and Suvla was completed. The evacuation of Helles was conducted from late December until 9 January 1916. The operation evacuated more than 140,000 men with negligible casualties and was easily the most successful element of the entire Gallipoli campaign.

Page 35

More than 1 million Indians, including Gurkhas, Afghans and Sikhs, fought in the British Indian Army. The Indian Mule Cart Corps was a unit of this army brought to Gallipoli. The carts were able to be used along the coast, but for trips to the front line supplies and water were loaded onto the backs of mules. The hardy animals also transported the wounded and were in constant demand.

Pages 36–37

 The first large contingent of wounded Australians landed at Fremantle on 9 July 1915 aboard the *Kyarra*. Thereafter, growing numbers of sick and wounded soldiers returned to Australia. Official telegrams notifying the next of kin of a soldier's return contained only general descriptions of injuries sustained, and it was common for soldiers to keep their letters home reassuring and cheerful.

Page 38

 The work of marking graves and burying the unburied dead was begun in 1918 by British Graves Registration personnel, and in the Anzac sector it was overseen by an Australian Gallipoli veteran from Tasmania, Lieutenant Cyril Emerson Hughes (1889–1958). In November 1919 Hughes was appointed Director of Works in control of the Imperial War Graves Commission's (now Commonwealth War Graves Commission) cemetery and memorial construction program on Gallipoli.

Page 39

 George Lambert's painting, *Anzac, The Landing, 1915,* is the largest painting in the Australian War Memorial collection. Lambert travelled to Gallipoli in 1919 with the Australian Historical Mission (headed by C.E.W. Bean) to make oil sketches for the painting. His words are taken from the manuscript of his autobiography held in the Mitchell Library, Sydney.

Pages 40–41

 Today on Gallipoli there are 31 war cemeteries, 21 of them in the Anzac area, containing 22,000 graves. Of these, only 9,000 are identified burials with grave markers. There are 5 memorials to the missing, the largest of which are at Lone Pine and Helles. The New Zealand National Memorial is at Chunuk Bair. (See Note for pages 28–29.)

Pages 42–43

 Pilgrimages of Australians and New Zealanders to Gallipoli became popular in the 1980s, probably as a result of Peter Weir's 1981 film, *Gallipoli*, and numbers have continued to increase over the decades.

Page 44–45

 In 1916, Australian forces in France, Egypt and Britain held services commemorating the Anzac landing. Today Anzac Day is a public holiday in all Australian states and is commemorated with dawn services and marches by returned servicemen and women – and, increasingly, their families.

The phrase 'We will remember them' is the last line of 'The Ode of Remembrance', from the poem 'For the Fallen', by Laurence Binyon (1869–1943), written in the early days of WWI and used in Anzac Day and Remembrance Day commemoration services since the 1920s.

Bibliography

Ah Kow, Adelaide. *Anzac Padre*. London: Salvationist Publishing, 1949

Bassett, Joan. *Guns and Brooches*. Melbourne: Oxford University Press, 1992

Davidson, Leon. *Scarecrow Army*. Melbourne: Black Dog Books, 2005

Commonwealth of Australia. *Gallipoli and the Anzacs*. Canberra: Department of Veterans' Affairs, 2010

De Vries, Susanna. *Australian Heroines of World War One*. Brisbane: Pirgos Press, 2013

Fewster, Kevin (ed.). *Bean's Gallipoli*. Sydney: Allen & Unwin, 2007

Gammage, Bill. *The Broken Years*. Canberra: ANU Press, 1974

Larsson, Marina. *Shattered Anzacs*. Sydney: UNSW, 2009

Starke, Ruth and Holfeld, Greg. *An Anzac Tale*. Adelaide: Working Title Press, 2013

Young, Margaret. *We Are Here, Too*. Adelaide: Australian Down Syndrome Assoc. Inc., 1991

www.awm.gov.au